Myths and Legends from Ghana
for
African-American Cultures

Myths and Legends from Ghana
for
African-American Cultures
as remembered by Rute Larungu
and pictured by Lou Turechek

A LOVEGIFT FOR A CHILD

TELCRAFT®

PRAISE AND THANKS: to Elizabeth Leadbeater, who helped me combine memory and research to recapture faithfully the words of the storyteller; to Joseph Campbell and Bruno Bettleheim, who convinced me that our lives are as nothing without the lovegift of myths and legends; to Doctors Ampofo, Bandoh, Rattray, Linton, and Wingert, who set me on a scholarly path; to many African artists, who enhanced my visual concepts; to my publisher and my artist, who have stood by me; and to all the tellers of and listeners to stories—especially my sister and my daughter and granddaughter—without whom there would be no storytellers, not even a story . . .

. . . from Rute Larungu.

Telcraft Books
Mogadore, OH 44260
Text copyright © 1992 Rute Larungu
Illustrations copyright © 1992 Lou Turechek
All rights reserved
Published in Mogadore, Ohio, by Telcraft Books
Printed in the United States of America
93 94 95 96 97 – 9 8 7 6 5 4 3 2
Type set in Goudy Old Style, printed on acid-free paper,
meeting the guidelines for permanence and durability
of the Committee on Production Guidelines for
Book Longevity of the Council on Library Resources.

Publisher's Cataloging In Publication
(Prepared by Quality Books Inc.)

African-American cultures : myths and legends from Ghana for / as
    remembered by Rute Larungu ; pictured by Lou Turechek.
p. cm.
ISBN 1-878893-20-3 (pbk.)
ISBN 1-878893-21-1 (Library Binding)
1. Ashanti (African people)--Africa, West--Legends. 2. Ashanti (African people)--Africa, West--Mythology. 3. Hausa (African people)--Africa, West--Legends. 4. Hausa (African people)--Africa, West--Mythology.
I. Larungu, Rute, 1917- II. Turechek, Lou.

DT471.M9 1992   996.3385
                                        92-81116
                                        QB192-515

Dedication

The stories in this book have been gathered from the folklore of the Ashanti and Hausa peoples of western Africa. Their homeland is in the "hump" of that great continent, where the coastline runs from the west to the east, right before it turns to run north and south again.

The legends tell the beginnings of both peoples; the myths reveal some of their early concepts of human behavior.

We people, known as Americans, are many kinds of people. Our roots reach far back into various cultures throughout the world. Whenever we find that the art forms (such as, music, dance, stories, paintings, designs, clothing) of our particular culture or cultures touch our lives, we respond to an added personal dimension.

So, we turn now to the many Americans who claim roots reaching far back into Africa. And because of the pride with which African Americans respond to that part of their ancestral background, the grandmother person who has remembered these myths and legends rightly presents them as belonging to *African-American Cultures*.

This book is dedicated to the differences that unite us and make us strong.

Acknowledgments

"No person alone with only two hands
can cover the whole of heaven."

If you are moved in some way–to laughter or
tears or curiosity, or to a better understanding–
by the words and pictures in this little book,
then join with us in giving praise and thanks to
those "metaphor makers" past and present,
whose messages we have herewith enfolded and
now pass on to you in this lovegift.

Contents

WORDS ABOUT PRONUNCIATION

Every letter is pronounced.

Exception: Hausa (HOW-zah)

Accent the next-to-last syllable.

Exception: baobab (BAY-oh-bab)

Practice:

Ananse (ah-NAN-say)

Anotchi (ah-NOT-chee)

Ashanti (ah-SHAN-tee)

Bornu (BOR-new)

Daura (dah-OOR-rah)

Denkyira (den-key-EAR-rah)

Kante (CAN-tay)

Kumasi (koo-MAH-see)

Malamai (mahl-ah-MY-ee)

Nkorowa (en-koh-ROW-ah)

Osai (oh-SAY-ee)

Sasabonsam (sah-sah-BON-sam)

Yiridi (YEAR-rid-dee) is the sound of someone running on a path. When you say it, say it however you think running along a path would sound.

LETTER ABOUT LOVEGIFT STORIES

Dear Gentle Reader:

Greetings to you from Rute Larungu. This letter is for you, whether you are very young or very old or somewhere in between.

You see, before you read these stories or someone reads them to you, I think you should know why myths and legends are so special. I think you should know about storytellers.

Long ago, when people had words to talk to each other but only a few people knew how to write down words or read them, certain people would remember stories and tell them. These people were called "storytellers." Storytelling was their profession.

And because storytelling was a profession, a storyteller could be a person of any age, a man or a woman. Yet, as it happened, storytellers in West Africa were mostly women, often the grandmother persons of the tribe. Of course, storytellers were not the only people who told stories, but storytellers were the ones who tried to be careful to tell the stories exactly as they had heard them.

When I was young and lived in Ghana (then called the Gold Coast), I heard stories from many different storytellers. Now I, too, am a grandmother person, and in thinking about these stories, I find that some of them have stayed in my memory very well—eight stories, to be exact—probably because they were my favorites. Three of them are Hausa stories and five are Ashanti stories.

And because they were lovingly told to me long ago, I have put them in this little book so that I can pass them on as *lovegifts* for you.

Stories can be lovegifts for many reasons. Some lovegift stories are told just to be silly, to amuse us, to make us laugh. Some are told to make us brave and strong. Some are called cautionary stories because they caution us: they give off a warning signal to keep us safe from harm.

Some stories try to explain the wonders of nature, like what causes the thunder. You know, when people don't have scientific ways to investigate nature, they have to imagine what causes something to happen as it does or to be the way it is. And they turn whatever they imagine into a story.

Many times, stories begin with a problem to be solved, and people or animals or gods (or whatever) in the story may be very wise or very foolish as they try to solve the problem. These stories give us a better understanding about the problems in our own lives so that we can be wise and not foolish when we solve our own problems.

All the things that happen in lovegift stories happen in myths. Myths usually start with some problem or some terrible trouble. They have good guys and bad guys: heroes who try to solve the problems and villains who only make more problems. In myths that are lovegifts, the hero gets a reward and the villain is punished.

Wild things happen in myths, the way they do in fantastic dreams or nightmares. Truly, myths are said to come from dreams—far-out dreams that were dreamed by people many years ago and told to other people as stories that really happened. The next person telling the story might make it even more fantastic, and so on, until a professional storyteller would hear the tale. After that, the story would be told almost exactly as the storyteller had heard it. Then other storytellers would hear it and tell it over and over again, and it would become a myth.

As storytellers passed along certain myths from one generation to the next, these myths become folklore because everybody who grew up in that tribe or that country knew those stories and *believed* in them, that is, they used them as models for their own behavior.

And so, these myths became part of the common *roots* of the people. Today, if we want to understand people in a certain culture, if we want to know what is important to them, what values they have in common, we can find out a great deal about them from the myths their storytellers told.

Legends are myths, too, but they are more like history stories because in legends some of the story really did happen. For instance, in *The Coming of the Golden Stool*, the storyteller tells how the people of Ashanti formed their large and powerful kingdom; in *The Horse with the Golden Horn*, the storyteller tells about the beginnings of the Hausa people, that is, where they came from many, many years ago.

For those of you who are hearing or reading these stories for the first time and who may have some questions, I have given some explanations in letters to you, which I have put in this book to go along with the stories.

The artist who drew the pictures is Lou Turechek. Her pictures are supposed to give you ideas. So, please, feel free to imagine whatever you like and draw your own pictures and color them to suit yourself.

Both she and I hope that you will read the stories to yourself or to someone else, or listen while someone reads them to you, over and over again. We hope they will become favorite stories for you just the way they are for us.

Your friend,

Rute Larungu.

FIRST HAUSA STORY

The Horse with the Golden Horn

This story is about something that everyone has always
known from the time of his grandfather and grandmother;
a story given to the people by the Malamai—the learned
men and the elders.

If a stranger should ask of you saying,
"Where did the Hausa people have their beginnings?"
say to him: "Truly, their beginnings came from the
people of the Bornu,
in the Lake Chad region of Nigeria."

When you see a Bornu man, you will know him at once by
his tattoo marks:
one line down the forehead, along the bridge of the nose,
seven cuts on the right cheek, and six on the left.

In the beginning, it happened that the King of the Bornu
   had a magnificent stallion with a Golden Horn.
This horse did not neigh just any time, but only on
   Fridays, and the sound of his neighing was like the
          sound of a tornado.

Now, the King was so proud of this horse
   that he had a special house built for it.
He appointed a special man to care for this horse,
   and that man was called the Keeper of the Horse.

The King commanded that this horse was never to be
          ridden by anyone;
   no one was to mount him or to sit upon him.

And the King also gave orders to the Keeper of the Horse
   that this horse was not to be taken out and mated
          with any other horse.

For if, by chance, a foal of this wonderful horse
   was ever found at the house of any man in his kingdom,
   the King would seize that man and have his throat cut.

Now, the King had a son, and this son had a fine mare;
   but he longed for a Horse with a Golden Horn,
   a horse that would neigh only on Fridays,
   like the horse of his father, the King.

So the King's Son went to the Keeper of the Horse
   to try to persuade him to let the stallion mate with
          his mare;
   but the Keeper of the Horse turned him away,
   for he was afraid of the King's anger.

When the King's Son found that he could not persuade the
    Keeper of the Horse, he planned how he might tempt him.

First, he offered money, a thousand cowries,
    and said that, as soon as it was dark,
        he would be waiting with his mare in a secret place
            in the forest.

Well, the Keeper of the Horse thought about it,
but he did not bring the Horse with the Golden Horn;
    instead, he came alone to return the cowries
    and to tell the King's Son, for the second time,
    that he was afraid to do this thing.

The next morning, while the King's Son was again
    thinking how he might tempt the Keeper of the Horse,
    he looked down upon the rich fabric of the robe he,
            himself, was wearing:
    cloth woven by the King's own weaver.
Surely, this was the one treasure desired by all men!

At last, the King's Son was full of hope,
    for now he knew how he could get the horse he wanted.

He went, at once, to the King's Weaver
    and told him to make a cloth of many colors;
and when the cloth was ready, he had it fashioned
        into a fine robe.

This he took and spread before the Keeper of the Horse,
and said it could be his, if only he would lead the
stallion to that place in the forest.

The servant of the King felt the fine cloth
and looked upon its rich colors;
then, he slipped it over his head, and the deed
was as good as done.

In the black of night, the Keeper of the Horse silently
    led the King's Horse deep into the forest.
There the stallion united with the mare of the King's Son;
and only the King's Son and the Keeper of the Horse
                  knew what had taken place.

Things remained at this
    until one day the mare gave birth to a fine colt.

Nothing happened while the colt was very young;
   but on the day that the young horse became full grown,
   of a truth, there it was!
Like his sire, the King's Horse, this horse, too, had
               a Golden Horn!

That was not all.
On the following Friday, when the King's Horse neighed,
   the young horse heard him, and he answered.

Well, the sound of this neighing was like the sound
               of big tornado
   followed by the sound of a little tornado.

The King's Son heard, and trembled!
The Keeper of the Horse heard, and trembled!
The King heard and rose up, and great was his anger,
   for now he knew that there must be another horse
               like the King's Horse.

And he said,
"At whose ever house you find it, let that person be killed!
Cut him down at once!
Do not let him be brought before me!"

So the councillors scattered to make a search in the town.
(They were searching for a Horse with a Golden Horn.)

At last, they came to the house of the King's Son,
               and behold! there it stood—
a Horse with a Golden Horn, just like the King's Horse.

The councillors closed in upon the King's Son;
    and they said, "The King has commanded
    that we must seize you and cut your throat!"

Whereupon the King's Son lifted his sword
    and cut down two men—the remainder were scattered.
Then he mounted his young Horse with the Golden Horn,
        and fled out of town.

When the King heard this, he ordered that his son
    should be pursued and brought before him.
The whole town mounted their horses,
    and chased after the King's Son.

But they could not come up to him, for his horse
    was much swifter than any of theirs.
Only one horse could have overtaken him
    and that was the King's Horse.

As for the King's Horse, the King had given orders
    that his Horse with the Golden Horn
    was never to be ridden.
So it was that no one could catch the King's Son, and
        he escaped.

At length, the young man knew that he was free of those
        who had pursued him,
    and he continued to travel westward.

After many days, he entered the Land of the Daura
   in the northern region of Nigeria.
Here, he came upon a village,
   where he dismounted and rested.

Now, the people of this village were ruled by the
                    Daughter of the King of the Daura.
So beautiful was she that she had no equal in the town.

When the Son of the King of the Bornu
   saw this most desirable of all maidens,
   he followed her to her house.

As for the Daughter of the King of the Daura,
   when she looked upon the young stranger and his
               magnificent Horse with the Golden Horn,
   she knew, at once, that of all the men in the world,
   she had seen the one she wanted most to marry.

But instead of rejoicing, she was sad;
   for already, two of her kinsmen had asked for her
          in marriage,
   and she had promised to choose between them.

All the same, the young man and the maiden told each
          other of their love,
and they whispered to one another a plan whereby
   the young man from Bornu could surpass her kinsmen
   in a contest and claim her as his wife.

So, the Daughter of the King of the Daura assembled
her councillors.
She told them that, as she now had three suitors,
she would hold a contest;
and the man who won, she would marry.

The contest was to be held on Friday
at the great baobab tree in the market.
The three suitors were to mount their horses
and, one at a time, come charging up to the baobab
to show their skill.

When Friday came, everyone assembled in the marketplace.
The three suitors mounted their chargers
   and rode a good distance away from the baobab.

Now, the owner of the Horse with the Golden Horn
          had no fear.
   It was he who had told the beautiful maiden
   to be sure to hold the contest on Friday.
Only he knew the power of the sound his horse could make.

While the people watched,
   the first of the kinsmen galloped swiftly,
   came upon the baobab,
   and thrust that tree with his spear.

The spear went right through the trunk of the tree,
          making a great hole;
   and he followed on his horse,
   passing through the hole made by his spear!
All the people were astonished!

The next kinsman came on charging.
When he was near the baobab tree,
   he lifted his horse on the bit, and jumped the baobab!
At this, the people were even more astonished!

Now it was the turn of the Son of the King of the Bornu.

First, he leaned forward and whispered in the ear of his
          Horse with the Golden Horn.
And because it was Friday, the horse neighed,
   and the sound was like the sound of a tornado.

So strong was the power of that sound as it surged round
              the trunk of the baobab,
    that it rocked that great tree from side to side.

Then the young man from Bornu came on riding at full speed.
As he was passing the baobab, he reached out,
    picked up the loosened tree, roots and all,
    held it aloft, and rode on, waving it!

The marketplace rang with the joyful sound of the guda,
    made by the people holding their noses
    and crying in shrill voices: *ruuu! ru! ru! ru!*

For there was no doubt who excelled among the
            three suitors.

So, the Daughter of the King of the Daura
    and the Son of the King of the Bornu were married;
    and many, many children were born to them.

This, then, was the beginning of the Hausa nation:
    the Bornu and the Daura are their ancestors.

That is all. Allah, he is the one who knows all.

LETTER ABOUT HAUSA STORIES

Dear Gentle Reader:

The Hausa people don't just say "hello" to each other; they say, "Greetings to you," and then they tell you whatever it is they see that you are doing.

If you are riding a horse, they say, "Greetings to you on a horse." If you are sitting under a tree, they say, "Greetings to you sitting under a tree." And so on. Well, then, I say:

"Greetings to you reading this book."

First, a word about baobab trees. Although baobabs are not tall, tall trees like the redwoods of California, they are almost as big around in the trunk (ten to twenty-five feet in diameter), and they are hundreds and hundreds of years old. Baobabs make homes for all different kinds of animals; they have an edible fruit (breadfruit), and they offer shade and protection during the hot, dry seasons. The baobab is famous.

Now, about legends. When we say that a legend is a story based on history and, therefore, partly true, we're not thinking about a horse leaping over a baobab tree, or a rider making a tunnel in it with his spear so that he and his horse can pass through, or a man picking up a tree with one hand and riding off with it. So much for fantasy—the spice of myth and also of legend.

The parts of this legend, *The Horse with the Golden Horn,* that are true are that the Hausa people are descendants of the Bornu (from Lake Chad in the northeast corner of Nigeria) and the Daura; also, that in certain tribes people are tattooed in a pattern to identify them as members of that tribe; that the Hausa are Muslims; and that the Malamai (mal-ah-MY-ee) are scribes, the elders of the tribe.

I have known the Hausa as a pastoral people of serene beauty and intelligence, who move their cattle across the African plains.

The cowries, mentioned in the story, are sea shells (marine gastropods), small and oval-shaped like a pecan. They make lovely beads. At one time they were so valuable that they were used as money. That was before gold dust was used as money in parts of Africa.

In the next two stories, the Hausa words at the beginning and the end of the story are traditionally said by the storyteller. And because the Hausa are Muslims, the Hausa storyteller would also begin a story with these words: In the name of Allah, the Beneficent, the Merciful; and end with these: Allah, he is the one who knows all.

What I remember best about the Hausa people is the Hausaman merchant who sold beautiful jewelry, useful and decorative artworks of leather, and warm blankets of camel's hair, strong enough to use as a rug. You could bargain with the Hausaman, and to whatever price you said first, he would say, "Hubba! Hubba!" which meant, "You gotta be kidding!"

Your friend,

Rute Larungu.

SECOND HAUSA STORY

"You may get a monkey out on a limb,
but be careful
it doesn't snap back on you."

What Makes the Thunder Roar

Gatanan, gatanan, ta je, ta komo.
A story, a story, let it go, let it come.

A certain man, when he came in from the bush,
    always brought with him a full tree.
When he came to his home, he would throw it down and say,
    "Ho! I am a man among men!"

His wife said, "Come now,
    leave off saying you are a man among men;
    for if you ever see a real Man Among Men,
    you will run."
But he said, "It is a lie!"

Now, it was always so: when he brought in wood,
   he would throw it down with force and say,
    "I am a man among men!"
His wife would say, "Come now, leave off saying so;
   if you ever saw a Man Among Men,
   you would run a mile."
But he would shout, "It is a lie! I am a man among men!"

One day when his wife went to get water,
   she came to a certain well and found the bucket so
   heavy that ten men would be needed to draw the water.
There was no one at the well to help her,
   and so she could not draw up the water.

The wife of the man who said he was a man among men
               turned to go home,
   when she met a large woman carrying a child on her back.
The large woman called out to her,
   "Where are you going with an empty calabash?
   Is there no water at the well?"

"There is much water at the well," she replied,
  "but I cannot draw up the bucket by myself."
The woman with the child upon her back said,
  "Let us return that you may get water."
So they returned together to the well.

Then the woman untied the child from her back
  and told him to draw water with the bucket.
The boy was small, not past the age when a child is
                    carried on the mother's back;
    but he lifted the bucket, then and there,
    put it in the well, and drew up the water.

The wife of the man who said he was a man among men
                    was astonished.

The women filled water pots;
  they bathed; they washed their clothes.
Then each woman filled a calabash with water,
  put it on her head, and prepared to go home.

Not long after they had been walking together on the path,
  the woman with the child on her back turned off the path
                    and started walking into the bush.
The wife said, "Where are you going?" and the large woman
  replied, "I am going home. Where else?"

She said, "Is that the way to your home?"
She said, "Yes."
She said, "Whose home is it?"
She said, "The Home of The Man Among Men."
  And the large woman and her son disappeared into the bush.

After this, the wife of the man who said he was a man
               among men was silent.
She did not say anything until she got home.

Then she told her husband, and he said that tomorrow
     she must take him and show him,
     for such a thing could not be.
He said, "We will go to the well tomorrow."
She replied, "May Allah give us a tomorrow."

The next morning he was the first to get up from sleep.
And he made ready: he took the weapons of the chase
     and slung them over his shoulder,
     put his axe on his shoulder, and awakened his wife.

She got up, lifted her large water pot upon her head,
               passed on in front,
     and he followed her to the edge of the well.
Now they found what they sought, indeed:
     the large woman was there, both she and her son.

They saw the bucket, and his wife said,
     "Go on, lift, and draw water for me."
So he went and lifted the bucket and put it down the well;
     but he would have fallen into the well,
     when the little boy seized both the man and the bucket,
     drew them out, and threw them to one side.

Now, once again, it was the boy who lifted up the bucket,
put it in the well, drew water, and filled their water pots.

Then the wife said to her husband,
"You have said you are going to see the one who is called
                    The Man Among Men.
    You have seen this one—this one is his son!
    If you still want to go, then go by yourself.
As for me, I am not going!"

The boy's mother said, "I warn you!
    You will be sorry. You had better not come."
But he said he would come.
    And she said, "Then let us be off."

When they arrived at the house, The Man Among Men
    was not home, so the woman hid him in a chest.
She said, "You stay there, and when my husband returns
    from the bush, you must not stir or make a noise."
And he stayed inside the chest till evening when the
                    master of the house came home.

This man was so huge that the floor and walls of the house
    began to shake with the weight of his body;
and as he sat down to his meal—ten elephants he could eat—
    his voice was like the sound of a tornado!
    "Ho!" he said to his wife, "I smell the smell of a man!"

His wife said, "Look around! Do you see another person?
    There is no one here but me.
    If you want to eat *me*, well and good."

Now, he that was hiding in the chest did not move
        and did not make a sound,
  but waited until he heard the giant snore,
  looked out, and saw that he slept soundly.
Then he stole away and fled into the bush.

He was running; he was running;
  until dawn, he was running;
  till the sun rose, he was running.

When the giant woke from his sleep, he said,
  "I smell the smell of a man! I smell the smell of a man!"
  And he rose up and followed where the man had gone.
Soon, the man who was running away could hear the
                    noise of him who was coming after.

As he ran, he met some people who were clearing the
                    ground for a farm.
They asked, "Why are you running?"
He said, "A giant is chasing me!"
They said, "Stand here till he comes!"

Soon they felt the rush of wind caused by the giant
                  as he came running after.
It lifted them and cast them down.

The man said, "This is the wind he makes when he runs.
  If you are able to withstand it, tell me;
  if you are not able, say so."
And they said, "Pass on!"

So he ran off until he met some people hoeing,
  but they, too, could not help him; and he passed on.
Next, he saw some people scattering seeds,
  but they could not withstand the giant; and he passed on.

Then he saw a man sitting alone at the foot
  of a baobab tree, roasting elephants he had killed.
As for this man, twenty elephants he could eat!
  His name was "The Giant of the Forest."

The giant said, "Where are you going in all this haste?"
The man said, "The Man Among Men is chasing me!"
The Giant of the Forest said, "Come here. Sit down
                till he comes."

Soon the wind made by The Man Among Men came and
    lifted the man and was about to carry him off.
The giant shouted, "Why are you leaving?"
The man said, "It is not I, myself, who is going off;
    the wind caused by The Man Among Men is taking me!"

With that, The Giant of the Forest got up and placed
    his hand upon the man's thigh, so the wind could not
                carry him off.

Thus they sat until The Man Among Men came upon them;
    and he said, "You! sitting there!
    Are you of the living or are you of the dead?"
The Giant of the Forest said, "You are interfering!"
The Man Among Men said, "If you want to find health,
    give me what you are keeping there!"
The Giant of the Forest said, "Come and take him!"

At that, The Man Among Men flew into a rage
    and sprang upon the giant and seized him.
As they struggled together, they twisted their legs
                around one another,
    and leaped up into the heavens.
Till this day, they are wrestling there.

When they are tired out, they sit down to rest;
    but when they rise up to struggle, that is the
              thunder we hear in the sky.

The other one, when he found himself escaped,
    went home and told the tale.
And his wife said, "That is why I was always telling you:
    whatever you do make little of it,
    whether you excel in strength or riches, it is all the same—
          someone is always better than you."

It is finished.
Kungurus kan kusu!
Off with the rat's head!

*"Because I fear I might be killed,
I have made my neck short."*

THIRD HAUSA STORY

"Just because you are hungry doesn't mean
you will get something to eat."

The Spider and the Terrible Great Ones

Gatanan, gatanan, ta je, ta komo.
A story, a story, let it go, let it come.

One time, there was a famine
    in that place where the Spider lived.
No food was to be found: not on the land nor in the water.
Of a truth, the Spider, his wife, and all his children
                were getting thin for want of food.

Things remained at this:
    the Spider searched but found no food,
    and he and his family were hungry.

One morning, he said to his wife,
    "Look sharp now! for I have a plan to get much food."
    "And what is your plan?" asked his wife.

The Spider replied, "As to that, you shall see.
I must go away, and while I am gone, here is your part:
    you and the children are to start twisting string,
    and whatever you do, do not stop twisting,
    for we shall need a great horse rope.

Remember, twist until I come back for you;
    then you and the children must go with me at once
                to get food. Tomorrow we begin."

"Very well," said his wife;
    and in the morning, after the Spider left,
    she and the children began to twist string.

As for the Spider, he hurried as fast as he could go
    along the path to the Elephant Chief's house,
    and the sound of his feet was like *yiridi, yiridi,*
                yiridi, yiridi.

Soon he came upon the Elephant Chief, resting under
                the Baobab Tree. Alone.
The Spider said, "Greetings to you, Great Chief,
    resting under the Baobab. May your life be prolonged."

The Elephant Chief said, "Speak, then, Spider."
The Spider said, "This very day have I come from
    the Court of the Hippopotamus, who sends you greetings
    and says I am to tell you that he has no grain."

The Elephant Chief, whose storage bins were full against
    the time of famine, said, "Hubba! hubba! no grain?"

"That is true, Great One," replied the Spider.
    "The Hippo says that if you will let me take back to him
    one hundred baskets of grain, when the harvest season
    comes, he will give you, in return, a great horse."

The Elephant thought about these words, and he said,
    "Very well, he needs the grain and in exchange he will
        give me a horse.
    That is a good bargain. Very well."

"There is one more thing," said the Spider.
"The Hippo says you must allow no one else to hear,
    since his promise of the horse is only for the ears
        of the Great Ones."

To this the Elephant Chief replied, "It is understood."

Then he called his young men and told them to take
    one hundred baskets of grain, follow the Spider
    to a place at the edge of the river, set down the
        grain, and return.

This they did, exactly as they were commanded.
After they had departed, the Spider hurried to his home,
    brought back his wife and children, and together
    they carried the grain off to their home.

At once, the Spider's wife made food, and the Spider,
    his wife, and all his children had a fine meal.

Early the next day, the Spider again set out
while his wife and children continued to twist string.
This time, the Spider hurried along to the river bank
and entered the water to call on the Hippopotamus Chief.

When found, the Hippo was sitting with his councillors.
The Spider approached and said, "Greetings to you,
Great Chief, seated among your councillors.
May your days be lengthened."

"Greetings to you, Spider," said the Hippopotamus,
and he asked, "What have you come to tell me?"
"I come with a message from the Court of the Elephant,"
replied the Spider, "but what I am to say is for the
ears of the Great Ones, only."

Upon these words, the Hippopotamus Chief dismissed his
councillors, and when they were alone, the Spider said,
"The Elephant Chief sends you greetings, and says that,
while he has plenty of grain, he has nothing with
which to make soup.

He would make a bargain with you: if you send him one
hundred baskets of fish, when the harvest season comes,
he will give you a great horse."

The Hippopotamus Chief thought and thought,
and at last he said, "That is a good bargain.
I will send him the fish, and later he will give me
a great horse."

"That is the bargain, Great Chief," said the Spider.
  And he made haste to add, "Remember, the Elephant
  says these words are for the ears of the Great Ones only.
He says, you must take care not to ask him anymore
                about this until the time comes."

The Hippopotamus Chief said, "I see no harm in that."
Thereupon, he called one hundred of his young men
  and told them to take on their heads a basket of
  fish each, and deliver all to the Elephant Chief.

So the Spider led the procession of one hundred men with
  their baskets of fish to a place on the river bank.

There he told them to set their baskets down.
  "For," he said, "the Elephant is sending his young men
    to carry the fish back to their chief.
These young men are said to be a quarrelsome lot;
  who knows what might happen when they come upon you?
It is better that you return home now and avoid trouble."

On hearing that, the Hippo's young men were glad to set
                      the baskets down. And they fled.
As soon as they were out of sight, the Spider ran to fetch
  his wife and children, who quickly took the baskets home.

And so, for many days, the Spider, his wife, and all
  his children were eating food and twisting string.
By the time the harvest season came, the rope was long
  and strong enough to reach from here to the sea.

Everything went according to the Spider's plan:
  one end of the horse rope he tied to a tree on the
  river bank, and the other end he took to the place
                      where the Elephant lived.

"The horse that the Hippopotamus is giving you
    is such a mighty beast," the Spider told the Elephant,
    "that the Hippo will not let him go until I return to
          tell him that the rope is secure."

So, he instructed the Elephant:
    "You must tie the rope to an enormous tree.
    When you see the tree start to shake,
    you will know that the horse is tied to the other end.
Then you must gather all your young men to take hold of
    the rope and pull the horse along the path."

Having done that part, the Spider hurried back to find
          the Hippopotamus Chief.

"Come!" he said,
    "the Elephant is ready to give you the horse!
    Send all your young men to the river's edge, at once!"

When they had gathered, the Spider said to the young men:
"Of a truth, this horse the Elephant gives your chief
          is the largest horse in the world.
You will need great strength to pull him along the path.
    Take the rope from the tree and start pulling, now!"

So the Hippo's young men pulled, and their pulling shook
    the tree to which the other end of the rope was tied.

At this signal, the Elephant's young men rushed forward,
  took hold of the rope, and pulled with all their strength.

On one end of the rope, the Hippo's people pulled.
On the other end, the Elephant's people pulled.
Until the sun was high, they pulled.
Until it sank low in the sky, they pulled.
                    Everyone was weary from pulling.

Then, as evening fell cool, the Elephant Chief said,
"Leave off pulling! This horse has worn out my people.
  We will send to the Hippo and see what kind of horse
              it is that he gives me."

Likewise, the Hippopotamus Chief told his people to
  cease pulling and go to the Elephant to see what kind
              of horse he was giving.

When the Hippo's young men returned,
  they told him that he owed the Elephant a horse.
When the Elephant's young men returned,
  they told him that he owed the Hippo a horse.
All was confusion.

"What's this?" cried the Elephant. "I owe nothing!
  The Hippo owes me! I gave grain for a horse!"
"What's this?" cried the Hippo. "I gave food for a great
  horse! The Elephant owes me! I owe nothing!"

Sleep did not come to the Elephant or the Hippopotamus
    that night, for they knew they had been tricked.
Everybody knows better than to trust the Spider.

In the morning, when things became visible,
    the Elephant sent to the Hippopotamus and said,
"Because we are both strong,
    the matter between us can never be settled.
Let us not be angry with one another.
Let us lie in wait for the Spider."

As for the Spider, he had not been waiting around.
He knew that, sooner or later, the terrible anger of the
                      Great Ones would come upon him.
Before the pulling began, he and his family *went for bush*,
    and for many moons, they had not been seen.

One day, the Spider thought he saw an Antelope,
    but all he saw was the skin, the head, and the hoofs.
               Some creature had eaten all the rest.

Now, the Spider had grown weary of hiding, and he saw
    that this antelope skin would make a fine disguise.
So he lifted up the skin, went inside,
    and wearing this disguise,
      he came out from the bush and walked along the path.
He had not gone far when he met the Elephant Chief.

The Elephant looked upon the Antelope, and he thought:
  What a decrepit, old Antelope!
  He is about to waste away, I do believe.
All the same, I will ask him if he has seen the Spider.

Then he said aloud,
  "Greetings to you on your coming from the bush, Antelope.
  Tell me, have you, by any chance, seen the Spider?"

From inside the antelope skin, the Spider made his voice
                very weak, and he said,
  "If you seek the Spider, keep that your secret.
  As for me, I wish never to see him again.
  We had an argument, and he pointed his finger at me.
  Since that time, I have wasted away.
  But I will tell all those I meet that you, the Elephant,
                are looking for the Spider."

The Elephant said,
"No, no, Brother Antelope, you have it all wrong.
  I am not the one looking for the Spider.
Forget I ever mentioned it!" And he hurried home.

The Spider watched the back of the Elephant disappearing,
  then he quickly got out of the antelope skin
  and hid it in the underbrush.

Yiridi, yiridi, the Spider ran down the path after the
  Elephant, and stood in front of him blocking his way.
  "Great chief! Behold! it is I, the Spider!" he cried.
  "I hear you are looking for me."

The Elephant began to tremble. "Not I!" he said.
    "I am not looking for you. Who told you that?"
And he went crashing across the fields to his home.

So the Spider went back to where he had hidden the
    antelope skin, and once more, put it on.
This time he fell in step with the Hippopotamus Chief.

The Hippo looked upon him. "Greetings to you, Antelope,"
    he said, "What a poor creature you are!
    How far have you traveled?
    Perhaps you have seen the Spider?"

Speaking in his thin, weak voice, the Spider answered:
    "The Spider? I do not wish to hear his name.
Nowadays, the Spider points his finger at anyone who
    quarrels with him, and that person begins to wither away!
    That is what happened to me.
But I will tell everyone
    that you are looking for the Spider."

The Hippopotamus said, "You have misunderstood, Antelope.
    Do not tell anyone that I am seeking the Spider.
    I was asking for someone else."
And the Hippopotamus moved along quickly to the river.

Once more, the Spider threw off the antelope skin,
    and moved as fast as he could to catch up with the Hippo.
He called,
    "Hippopotamus Chief, I hear you are looking for me.
    Here I am! What is it you want?"

This action so startled the Hippopotamus that he lost
   his balance, and fell with a splash into the river.

So it was that the Spider saved himself, his wife,
   and all his children, from starvation.
So it was, too, that the little Spider tricked the
                   Terrible Great Ones.

It is finished.
Kungurus kan kusu!
Off with the rat's head!

"If the little fish says the crocodile is dead,
you had better believe him."

FIRST ASHANTI STORY

The Coming of the Golden Stool

Let the voice of the drums stop talking;
let them now be silent.

Draw near and listen to my story, O my people;
but you, O Sasabonsam, and all you evil spirits,
                stay away!
  You cannot come to touch me nor harm me
  for the words of my mouth;
for hear! I say,
  "I do not really mean, I do not really mean."

Long ago in the land that is now the Kingdom of Ashanti,
  there were seven different kingdoms,
  and each kingdom had its own king.

These kings did not live in peace, one with the other,
    but many times, made war;
      and the weak kings were conquered by the strong.

One of these weak kings was the King of Kumasi,
    and he was conquered by the King of Denkyira.
Now, the people of Kumasi,
    living together there in the forest, were held captive.
To make certain that they did as they were told and
              gave no trouble,
    the King of Denkyira took the little boy
    who was next in line to the King of Kumasi,
    the little boy who was, one day, to be King of Kumasi.

That child was held hostage;
and if the people of Kumasi gave the Denkyira trouble,
    of a truth, the King of Denkyira would kill that
             little boy.
That boy was called Osai Tutu.

Things remained at this:
Osai Tutu lived among the people of Denkyira;
    but, as for that little boy, he was growing up.

Always he dreamed that one day his people of
              Kumasi would be strong again,
    so that he could return to his own kingdom.

Now, it happened that many times while Osai was listening,
    and he listened every chance he could get,
    he would hear the people telling stories about a
              great magician, a fetish priest,
    who lived in the Kingdom of Juaben.

This man was called Okomfo Anotchi.

And Osai listened to people telling
   how this Anotchi had made a study of the fetish.
They said that this man could put together in a box
   things to make strong, strong medicine.

Only Anotchi knew what things; but they said,
   "Things like the sharp nails from the right front paw
                  of the leopard,
   the hair from the head of the gorilla,
   tea leaves from the gardenia bush,
   and crocodile bile dried in the sun."

Around this strong medicine, people said that
               Anotchi would dance,
   and great was the magic he could perform.

Where there was no water for the land,
   he could cause the rain to come from the sky.
When people brought sick children,
   he could cause the evil spirits to go away for them.
When the hunter felt the claw of the lion, and his blood
             life came from him, Anotchi,
   he could make this blood stop.

And sometimes, a man—far away—Anotchi,
   he could cause that man to get a pain,
   and from the pain, that man would die.
This he could do and still be far away.

All the people knew the magic of Anotchi.

As for Osai Tutu, growing up,
 while he listened to these stories about Anotchi,
 he began to form a plan to save his people.

He knew, one day, he would be old enough to run away;
and when he was old enough,
 he would go to find this great magician,
 and he would ask Anotchi to help him return to
        Kumasi and make his people strong.

This, then, was exactly what Osai Tutu did.

One morning, very early, before things became visible,
   he slipped way from his captors, took to the bush,
      and traveled many, many days.

Then, one day, as evening fell cool,
   he came to the Kingdom of Juaben;
there, he sought out Anotchi.

But when found, Anotchi surprised Osai.
As soon as he saw the young man, he rose up and said,
   "Greetings to you on your coming, Osai Tutu!"
Of a truth, Anotchi had been expecting Osai;
   for Anotchi talked many times to the Sky God,
   Onyame—that is how he knew about Osai.

The message Anotchi received from Onyame was that one
    day there would be a powerful kingdom called Ashanti,
    and this very Osai Tutu was to be its king.

That is how it happened that Anotchi treated Osai Tutu
    just like the great king he knew one day he would be.

Always when they went, they would go together:
    Anotchi was the right hand of the young man,
    and he taught Osai many things to make him strong.

They continued thus in the Kingdom of Juaben
    until it happened that the King of Kumasi died.
When news of this reached Osai Tutu,
    he knew he must go to Kumasi because he was next in
            line to be the king.

So these two went together, this Osai Tutu and Anotchi,
    and they ruled the people of Kumasi
    and made them strong—so strong that other kingdoms
            did not trouble them.

One day, Anotchi, talking to Osai Tutu,
    told him of the Sky God's plan:
    "The time has come," he said, "for all the people of
            Ashanti to be united."

And this was how it was to be:
The seven kings of the seven kingdoms of Ashanti
    would meet in Kumasi to hold a big palaver.
Each king would bring the stool of his kingdom,
    and Anotchi would take these seven stools
    and put all, together, in one place.

Then, with the help of Onyame,
he would cause a flame to come out of the sky,
   and it would set fire to these stools, and they
          would burn.

Then the smoke would go up,
   and out of this smoke would come a golden stool,
   and it would descend until it came to rest upon the
          knees of the very man
  who would be king above all the other kings;
  indeed, the one who was to be the first King of Ashanti.

And although he knew, Anotchi did not tell anyone,
  not even Osai Tutu, who that man would be.

So Anotchi made the preparations.
He went on a long journey, visiting each kingdom to tell
          the people of the Sky God's plan,
  the same plan he had told Osai Tutu.
After Anotchi had traveled for many moons,
  he returned to Kumasi.

At last the appointed day of the palaver came.
On the morning of that day,
  as soon as things became visible,
  the voice of the drums could be heard across the land.

Many, many people gathered together,
  and they formed a great circle in the clearing in
          the forest.

Each king, dressed in fine Kante cloth,
    sat on a throne under his own big umbrella—colors of
        red, green, gold, and blue.
There they were with their people and many valuable things.

As for each king and the stool he had brought,
these stools were put together in one place.

When all was made ready, Anotchi commenced his magic:
    there, in the center of the great circle,
    he placed his box of strong medicine;
    and as the rhythm of the drums became faster and faster,
        Anotchi danced round and round.

At length, behold! a flame came from the sky, and it
        went among the stools,
    winding in and out; and they began to burn.

All the people said, "Ahhhh!"

And the stools, burning there together, formed the smoke.
    Black, black it was, and it rose up to the sky.
Then Anotchi called to Onyame, the Sky God,
    and the people heard great rumblings.

While they looked at the smoke, they saw a black shape
    like a stool coming from the smoke in the sky;
    and it came down—floating it was—through the air.

Then the people drew back the umbrellas from over the
    heads of the kings, so that the stool could find the
        knees of the one it sought.
And they waited and watched.

As they watched that black stool come slowly floating,
  not a sound could be heard—
  even the forest was silent.

At last, the stool came to rest,
and it rested on the knees of Osai Tutu.

While the eyes of all the people were on that black stool,
    the blackness began to go away.
Little by little, as the people watched,
    they could see that the stool was made of solid gold.
And it shone in the sun!

No one dared speak but Osai Tutu.
Then he spoke to Anotchi, and Anotchi spoke to the people.

He told them that they were all now united,
    that never again would they make war one with another,
    that, from this day on, their kingdom would be
            called Ashanti,
    and that this man, Osai Tutu, was the King of Ashanti.

Then all the people made the noise of joy.
So loud it was that the trees of the forest shook with
            the sound of it.

When the great noise ceased and all was quiet again,
    Anotchi lifted the Golden Stool of Ashanti from the
            knees of Osai Tutu
    and placed it upon a white cushion made of woven silk.
And he asked Osai Tutu to stand, there,
    with his back to the stool.

Then Anotchi chose two men, and told them to stand
    one on each side of Osai Tutu and support his arms
    so that they could lower him very carefully over
            the Golden Stool.

This they were to do so that the shadow of his body would
   fall across the stool, but he would not sit upon it.

This they did, and afterward Anotchi told the meaning:
In the Golden Stool of Ashanti
   dwells the spirit of the people of Ashanti.
While the king reigns, the shadow of his wisdom will
                     fall upon the people,
   but he must never oppress them—
   he must not sit upon them.

No one anywhere in the world must ever sit upon the
                  Golden Stool of Ashanti.

And from that very day to this,
   when the King of Ashanti dies
   and a new king comes to take his place,
that is how he is made king.

So it was that the seven kingdoms all came together
   to form the great Kingdom of Ashanti.
No one has ever conquered the Ashantis,
   and no one anywhere in the world has ever sat upon
                     the Golden Stool.

This my story, which I have told you,
   if it be sweet, or if it be not sweet,
take some with you and let some come back to me.

LETTER ABOUT ASHANTI STORIES

Dear Gentle Reader:

Greetings to you, again, from me, Rute Larungu. This time, my letter to you is about the Ashanti stories in this book. When you have finished reading this letter, I hope that you will know more than you know now.

Let's begin with *Words about a storyteller's words.* I'm sure you have noticed that storytellers everywhere often say a few words before they get on with their story. It's the same for African storytellers, especially when the talking drums have been booming out a message telling people to gather around, take their places, and get ready to listen.

That's when the storyteller has to tell the drums to be quiet. Otherwise, nobody could hear what she has to say. "Let the voice of the drums stop talking," she begins.

Then, because the storyteller believes that trouble comes from evil spirits, she has to call out to the king of evil spirits, the *Sasabonsam.* (*Sasa* is the word for ghost; *bonsam* is anything evil.)

She has to tell him to call off all his evil spirits and not let them pick on her because of something in the story to which they might object. She says that, after all, she doesn't really mean what she is saying; she's only repeating what she heard from somebody else.

Words about talking drums. Now, the drums she tells to be quiet are a pair of large talking drums, called *atumpan* in Ashanti. One of them has a low voice and the other has a high voice. What the drummer does with these two drums is this: he plays them so that they imitate the pitch in human voices.

These drums probably wouldn't amount to much where the language spoken is English, but they're the whole show where people speak *Akan* or some other "tonal" language.

To speak a tonal language, you have to be sure to say a word at the right pitch—high or medium or low, rising or falling. That's because, as you change pitch, you change meaning: the same word can mean something entirely different depending on the highness or the lowness of its sound.

A really good atumpan drummer with only two drums can get the pitch to sound so perfect that, to people who know the language, the drums are talking.

Words about the next in line to be king. In the story about the Golden Stool, Osai Tutu is said to be "next in line to the King of Kumasi"; in other words, he was the appointed person who was to become king when the king died.

We usually think of the person who will become king when the king dies as being the king's son (the prince) or,

perhaps, the king's daughter (the princess) because, in many parts of the world, royal lineage passes from the parent to a child. (Remember, in the *First Hausa Story*, the people in the village were ruled by the Daughter of the King of the Daura.)

But in this Ashanti story, royal lineage for Osai Tutu meant that he had to be the king's *nephew*, not his *son*; that is, he had to be the son of the king's sister.

The Ashanti storyteller doesn't tell you that Osai is the king's nephew and not his son because, if you had been living there and listening to the story, you'd *know* that. Well, *now* you know.

Also, if you had been living there, you'd know that a *queen mother* is never the *wife* of a king—she is a *sister* of the king. She becomes a queen mother when the king (her brother) dies and her own son becomes king. A queen mother is the *mother* of a king.

Words about families and tribes. Remember that when these stories were told years ago the people lived in tribal societies. If you had lived in that place at that time, all people in your parents' generation would be "mother" or "father" to you, and all people in your generation would be regarded by them as being their children.

It would be the same with grandparents. All the older people in the tribe would be "grandmother" or "grandfather" to you, and you would be "grandchild" to them. Nonetheless, everybody knew who his or her *real* parents were or which children were their *real* children. And they would say so when they spoke of them.

Words about Kante cloth. On the back cover of this book, you will see a picture of what Kante cloth looks like. It is beautiful cloth and very costly, being made by hand in narrow strips (about three inches wide) of heavy silk or cotton threads in many colors.

After these strips have been woven, they are sewn together. You can see in the picture where they were sewn together. Because of the way they are made, every Kante cloth is different.

To make a Kante cloth, the weaver uses a small loom about twelve inches wide, which rests on a table in front of him. On this loom he weaves his long strips, or ribbons. The very long threads that make the length of the cloth are the warp; the short threads that cross over the warp are the weft or woof.

If you look closely, you will see that the long warp pattern in each cloth always has the same stripes, while the weft patterns, which are made by the weaver as he passes the threads from side to side across the warp, are different in every section. Weaving such as this takes many, many hours to do. It is no wonder that a man's Kante cloth is often his prize possession.

True Kante cloth is never cut and sewn together to make a garment. It is always worn as a whole cloth, which is wrapped around the body leaving only the right arm and shoulder bare.

When a man puts on the Kante, he wraps it around his body so that one end lies over his left arm and shoulder and the other end passes under his right arm. Then, with his right hand, he takes up the end of the cloth which has passed under his right arm and artfully gathers it into folds and throws it over his left shoulder. There, after a slight adjustment, it stays, letting the folds hang gracefully down the front from his left shoulder to the floor.

Words about Ashanti stools and the Golden Stool. Here's a riddle for you: When is a stool not like any other stool in the world? And here's the answer: When it's an Ashanti stool, of course.

Other stools have legs. Some may be short stools like footstools. Some may be tall like step stools or stools at counters or stools on a stage where people sit to read from a book, recite poetry, or tell jokes. Ashanti stools are not like any of these.

For instance, Ashanti stools don't have legs, and they are custom-made to suit the height of some one person—the one who is to sit upon that stool.

Besides, Ashanti stools are not joined or fastened together anywhere; they are made by carving out a solid piece of wood. Furthermore, they have "ears"—small knobs on each side so you can get a grip on the stool to lift it or move it.

To make an Ashanti stool, the wood-carver starts with a block of wood, one which is the shape of a rectangular box. Using his wood-carver's tools, he allows for a curved seat at the top, which becomes the widest part of the finished stool; for a base at the bottom, which must be wide enough to support the finished stool; and for a narrower middle section where the "meaning" of the stool will be carved or sculptured.

The "meaning" of the stool is done in symbols, which can be like the ID of the person who owns the stool. The "meaning" may be a symbol indicating that this person is the head of family or the queen mother or the chief or any role that person may have. Sometimes the stool is carved with the symbols of a proverb, a saying, that expresses a person's personality or special interests.

It is best not to have to buy your own stool but to be given a stool by someone who loves or admires you—the person giving you a stool may have a special message designed for you in the symbol of the stool.

An old tradition at weddings is that the bridegroom gives the bride a stool to show that she now has a place in his life.

My Ashanti stool, given to me by students, has the symbol of the turn-around bird carved on it. The proverb is: *"Wisdom is knowing what to pick up from the past."*

They say that a person's soul rests in the stool the person uses during his or her life. When a person dies, that stool is supposed to be blackened (to preserve it) and put in a place with other ancestors' stools.

Tribes and kingdoms have stools, too. The stool of a tribe or a kingdom is the same to the people as the flag of a country: the symbol of loyalty and pride. It is said that the soul of the people dwells in the stool of that nation. So it is with the Golden Stool of Ashanti.

Words about a Spider. We know that stories come from many sources: from experiences and dreams, from imagination. I understand there was a time when people believed that all stories came from some *place.* They may have believed this because stories were not written down; they were told by one generation to the next.

Many years ago in Ashanti, people believed that the source of all stories was the Spider, who was called *Ananse.*

This they believed even when Ananse wasn't in the story at all. And because Ananse was the source of all stories, he was called Father Spider. In fact, the word for a story in Ashanti is *anasesem*, which means "words about a spider."

This, Gentle Reader, may be your first time of meeting Ananse, the Ashanti Spider. But I am sure you have met other important Spiders in stories from other cultures (like *Spiderman*, for instance). You know, for some reason, the same sort of story has a way of turning up in many different cultures, and the Spider is a prominent figure in the folklore of many countries.

Although, in the Ananse stories in Ashanti, the Spider often plays tricks and gets the better of people, the Spider in other folklore may not be like that. Sometimes he may be like a god, doing the impossible; or like a hero, solving great problems; or like every person, having trouble just the same as you and I do.

The next story in this book is about Father Spider and his young son, Ntikuma (pronounced en-tee-KUH-mah). There is a saying: No one tells stories to Ntikuma. If you say, "What else is new?" or "Tell me about it!" you are saying the same thing. You see, since people believed that all stories came from Father Spider, he would most certainly have told them to his own child. So what else is new?

Well, I do hope, Gentle Reader, that you know more now than you did before you read this letter. Unless, like Ntikuma, you've heard it all before. Which could be true, of course.

Your friend,

Rита Laringu.

SECOND ASHANTI STORY

How Wisdom Came to the Tribe

It happened that Ananse, who is Father Spider,
    had been traveling for many moons;
    he had gone to the ends of the earth.
And every time he found a bit of wisdom, Ananse shut it
    up in the special gourd he carried for that purpose.

Ananse had labored long and hard to gather all the
    wisdom in the world and bring it back to the tribe.

Now, he had only one thing left to do:
    climb the tallest tree in the marketplace
    and scatter wisdom upon the people.
His plan was to do this so that ever after wisdom
                would be found in the tribe.

Holding the gourd in one hand, Ananse began to climb.
So far and no further could he go
   for he was greatly hindered by his load.

Ntikuma, his little son, stood nearby watching.
  "Father Spider," he called to him, "why do you not tie
                the gourd to your back,
  then you would have both hands free to climb?"

Well, Ananse listened to his son and tied the gourd
  to his back, and he was soon at the top of the tree.

There, he sat wearily upon a limb;
and he said, "Eeee! what is the use!
  I have searched long and hard to gather
  all the wisdom in the world to give to the tribe,
and now, even my own small son gives me some wisdom
        I did not have!"

All the same, Ananse reached into the gourd,
  and bit by bit, he scattered what wisdom he had.

Of a truth, that is how wisdom came to the tribe—
  some wisdom, that is, but not all.

THIRD ASHANTI STORY

The Nkorowa Dance

A certain Night Jar bird was very fond of dancing.
When his friends came by to take him along to the dance,
                    what could he do but consent?

Now, this same Night Jar had a bean plantation
    where he labored day after day to grow his beans.
But always, when the time came to gather them,
                    he would find nothing—
    someone had come in the night and carried them off.

So the bird stood watch as each harvest drew near,
    except, of course, for the dance—then, off he would go.
Of a truth, he reasoned, if everyone is busy dancing,
                    no one will be stealing beans.

Well, everyone was busy dancing; but in the morning,
    when things became visible, the Night Jar could see,
    once again, his beans had been stolen. Every bean!

Now, Ananse the Spider was also very fond of dancing.
Both he and the Night Jar were particularly fond
    of the Nkorowa dance, for one or the other of them
        was always chosen to lead it;
    often, they would argue over which one was to lead.

One night, to his surprise, the Night Jar noticed that Ananse,
    along with many others, was coaxing *him* to be the one
        to lead the Nkorowa.

Now, the Night Jar was pleased not to have to argue,
    but as he began to lead the dance,
    he remembered what everyone knows: Ananse the Spider
        is a crafty fellow.
Then, at that very moment, he thought about his beans.

So, while he lead the dance, he kept an eye on Ananse;
sure enough, at the height of the dance,
    while everyone was twirling and leaping,
    the Night Jar saw Ananse slip away.
Early in the morning, as he feared, his beans were gone!

For many days, how to outsmart this crafty Spider
    occupied the mind of the Night Jar bird.
He thought and thought, and hit upon this plan:
    first, he made a clay model of himself,
    plucked out some of his feathers,
    and stuck them in the model.

The next time the beans were ready to harvest,
   he put the model in the middle of the plantation,
   and off he went, merrily to the dance.

When the time to dance the Nkorowa came, he was not
   surprised to find Ananse pleading that he,
   the Night Jar, be the one to lead it.
And, as before, at the height of the dance, Ananse
               slipped away.

Imagine Ananse's surprise when he spied the Night Jar,
   there, in the middle of the beans.
Ananse ran back quickly to join the dance,
   and behold! there was the Night Jar leading the dance.

Off he slipped to the beans once more,
   but there was the Night Jar!
   So, once more, back to the dance.

Enough of this, said Ananse to himself,
    as he walked right up to the Night Jar bird.

Stopping the dance, he said,
    "My advice to you, Night Jar, is this:
      if you are supposed to be leading the Nkorowa,
        then lead it, but if you are supposed to be watching
                the beans,
      then give your time to that!"

As for the Night Jar, who had found a way to do both,
    he smiled and said nothing.
And that is why, before going to the dance,
    the Night Jar always leaves a model of himself in
            the bean patch.

Words about advice. Did you notice that the kind of
advice Ananse gave the Night Jar was the kind that
would help Ananse, himself, not the Night Jar? AHA!

FOURTH ASHANTI STORY

"On the honeymoon,
the yams always taste sweet."

How the Parrot's Tail Become Red

Draw near, my people, and listen to my story.
But you, O Sasabonsam, stay away!
    Of a truth, the words that I speak
    are the same as those that my grandmother before
        me spoke.

Once long ago, the Queen Mother bore a girl child.
When the child grew tall, there she was—
    beautiful to look upon, but in her nature, bold.

They say she would sit on her father's lap and declare:
    "As for me, there is nothing anywhere I fear."
    To this, her father would say, "Just you wait and see!"

The time came for the Queen Mother's Child to marry.
　　But when they gave this beautiful maiden in marriage
　　　　　　　　to anyone, she refused to marry.
Many people would go to her and speak about marriage,
　　but always she would say, "Certainly not!"

Now, the creature Onini the Python lived in the bush.
　　His home was there in a cave.
One day, he heard some hunters passing by his cave,
　　and they were talking about the Queen Mother's Child—
　　about how, when she was given in marriage to anyone,
　　　　　　　　she did not want him.

The Python lay there, curled up in his cave,
　　and he said to himself: Ho! what is this?
　　A maiden who will not marry?
I will change myself into a fine young man. She will
　　　　　　　　not refuse *me!*

Of a truth, then and there, the Python changed himself
　　into a youth so beautiful that to gaze upon him long
　　　　　　　　was not possible.
　　Then he set out for the village.

As he went along, he was chewing kola nuts and making
　　　　　　　　up a song with his voice.
Upon reaching the village, he looked to see
　　if the Queen Mother's Child was out and doing.

Now it happened that she had gone early to beat the
　　washing but had returned, and at that moment,
　　she was spreading the clothes out to dry.
So there she was, her back to the handsome young man.

The young man walked up to her
   and spat upon the back-skirt of beads she was wearing.
The maiden turned, and seeing this young man of great
                      beauty, she spoke:
  "Why do you spit on my back-skirt?"

The young man said, "You do well to ask, Amu."
She said, "My nton salutation is not Amu."
He said, "You do well to ask, Eson."
She said, "My nton salutation is not Eson."
He said, "You are right in saying so, my wife."
She said, "Does that mean I have married you?"
He said, "If you wish."

Thereupon, the Queen Mother's Child
    and the fine young man set off together for her house.
As they came running, the maiden was so excited
    she could hardly talk. "Eh! eh! eh!" she stammered.
    "Look, mother, here is the one I desire!"
The Queen Mother said, "Well, at last!"

So, the Queen Mother extended her hand in welcome
    to the young man, and as he took her hand, she said,
    "Let me look at my son-in-law."
And he said, "Here I am, Grandmother."
    The Queen Mother said, "May you and your wife live
                together happily."

And so it was that, when evening fell cool,
    the young man and the Queen Mother's Child went to rest.
Thus they lived, this husband and wife,
    in the village of the Queen Mother for eight days.

The next morning, the husband said, "My wife,
    I am going to my village, but I shall soon return."
She said, "Then you and I shall go together."
He said, "No." But she would not listen.
    So these two set out together along the path.

At length, the husband branched off the path and took
    to the bush, so the Queen Mother's Child followed.
And she called to him, "What are you doing, my husband?
                Is this the path to your village?"

"As for you," he replied, "shut your mouth and do as
        you're told!" So on they went.
Suddenly, the young man disappeared into a cave.
    The Queen Mother's Child looked in and followed.

There in the dark she could see nothing,
    and she slowly turned around.
    "Where did you go?" she called out.
Then, between herself and the light at the entrance to
        the cave, she saw a huge beast.

It was the Python, himself.
And he moved close to her.
    The breath from his great mouth was hot upon her face.
    His eyes pierced into hers, and his slippery body
        coiled around her legs.

The beast hissed at her, "This is who I really am!
    Your husband is Onini the Python!
    I changed myself to marry you and teach you a lesson.
You used to sit on your father's lap and say
    that there was nothing you feared.
Well, now I shall kill you!
    Scratch my head and get the lice.
    If you don't get some, you are finished with food!"

The Queen Mother's Child was trembling with fear,
    but she began to scratch his head searching for lice.
There in the cave the two of them were:
    the Python holding her fast and the Queen Mother's
        Child scratching his head.

Then, she saw a parrot flying by the entrance to the cave.
    She was about to call out: Father Parrot, save me!
    when the Parrot stretched his eyes and shook his head
          to warn her to be quiet.

She saw the Parrot take his gun, and making it ready,
    he braced it against himself and took aim.
"You are not scratching!" cried the Python.
    "Scratch my head, I tell you!"
She said, "I am weary of scratching it.
    If you must kill me, then kill me!"

And just as the Python raised his head,
    the Parrot made the gun to cry out: POMM!
Onini the Python lay dead, and the Queen Mother's Child
          sank upon the floor of the cave.

So, the Parrot went into the cave to get the Queen
    Mother's Child and the dead Python and take them home.

There, he told the Queen Mother and all who had gathered
    together how he had seen the Python about to kill the
          Queen Mother's Child,
    and how he had killed the Python.
Also, the Queen Mother's Child told her story.

When all had been said,
    the Queen Mother turned to the Parrot, and she asked,
    "What must we do to thank you?"
The Parrot said, "Grandmother, I don't want anything;
          only bring some palm oil."

So the Queen Mother went out and returned with a
    calabash of palm oil and placed it before the Parrot.

Then, the Parrot told the meaning:
    "Grandmother," he said, "I am taking my tail and dipping
        it into this palm oil as a remembrance of this day."
And that is how the Parrot's tail became red.

This my story, which I have told you,
        some of it you may take as true;
        as for the rest, you may praise me for telling it.

Words about palm oil. When oil is squeezed from the
African oil palm, *genus Elasis*, it is deep, glossy red in color.

FIFTH ASHANTI STORY

"A woman who gives birth to a disobedient child
will grow tired of speaking."

Why Old Women Have White Hair

This my story, if it be sweet or if it be not sweet,
  take some with you, and let some come back to me.

In a certain village there was a woman who bore
              a girl child.
When this child grew big enough,
  her mother told her she must help with the work.

But every time the mother told her what to do,
  the child replied, "I shall not do it!"

When the mother sent her on an errand,
  the child would say, "I shall not do it!"
The mother said, "Then stay! you and your wise ways!"

One day the mother rose up in the morning and
   told the child to go splash water and bring for her.

Now, the mother was getting tried of speaking;
   so when the child said, "I shall not go!"
   she replied, "I am sick of you! I, myself, shall go!
   But just you wait and see!"

The child said to herself: What is Wait and See?
    I will go to search for Wait and See that I may see
        what it is like.

So she set off on the path at a great pace,
    and the sound of her feet running was like *yiridi,*
        yirdi, yirdi, yirdi.

Well, the child had never before been on the path
    that took her away from her village,
    and soon she was lost and frightened, and she began
        to cry.

At length, she arrived at the outskirts of a town,
    where she saw a certain old woman sitting under
        a coconut palm nearby.

The child made to draw back, but the old woman said,
    "Do not draw back, Grandchild, for I have seen you."

So the child came forward, and the old woman said,
    "Why has water from your eyes bathed you like this?"

"My mother and I live together over there," she said,
        pointing toward her village.
"When she rose up, she got angry with me, and she said,
    'Just you wait and see,' and she left me.

So I said I would come and search for Wait and See
        that I may see what it is.
Tell me, Grandmother, do you know Wait and See?"

"You have found it," said the old woman.
  "I am Wait and See!
  And that house, over there, is where I live."

Then she said, "Go to the back of the house, Grandchild,
                and dig up yams and bring for me.

When you go and reach there, the ones that say,
  'Dig me up! Dig me up! Dig me up!' do not dig those;
    but the ones that say, 'Don't dig me up! Don't dig me
                up! Don't dig me up!'
  those are the ones you may dig."

So the child went to the back of the house;
    and of a truth, certain of the yams said,
                "Dig me up!" Those she did not dig.
    But those that said, "Don't dig me up!" those she dug.
And she came with them to the old woman.

Then the old woman said, "Go gather wood for the fire."
    And she brought the wood for the fire.

Next, the old woman said, "Now you must skin the yams
                    and put them on the fire."

And she skinned them and put them on the fire,
    and when cooked, she turned them out into a calabash,
    and took and set them before the old woman.

The old woman said, "Go along the path to the town
    and look on a rack which has meat lying on it.
    Look among, and take your choice."

And the child did as she was told;
    she brought the meat, placed it on the fire, and
                made soup.

"It is time to pound the fufu," said the old woman;
    and she sat down upon the ground and told the child,
    "You must take the cooked yams and put them in my
                mouth and pound them."

The child said in her head: Here is something wonderful!
    Pounding fufu in a person's mouth!
    This must be Wait and See that mother talked about!

"Mark you," cried the old woman, "you must pound strongly!
    If you do not pound strongly, your chest will split!"

So she put the cooked yams in the old woman's mouth;
and taking the pounding stick in both hands,
the child stood over the old woman where she sat,
and she began pounding the yams in her mouth—
pi! pi! pi! pi!

When she had finished, she took the pounded fufu,
  put it with the soup, and set all before the old woman.
"Now, Grandchild," said the old woman,
  "first, you must mention my name, and then you may
              take food and eat."

The child said, "You are called Old Woman Grandmother."
"Eeeee!" said the old woman, "she has not seen the way
              to eat—she may not eat!"
And the old woman ate up all the food.
For eight days she treated the child thus, always.

One day the child went to the river to splash water.
The Crab saw her, and spoke to her.
  "Why has somebody's child got thin like this?" he asked.
And she told the Crab all.

She said, "I live with an old grandmother woman,
  and when I cook food and put it down, she says,
  'Mention my name and take and eat.'
I say, 'You are called Old Woman Grandmother,'
  and she says, 'Eeeee! you do not know the way to eat!'
  and then she takes all and eats it up.
              That is why I am thin."
And the child began to cry.

The Crab said, "That old woman! Why she is called
              Old Woman Key-key-ma-DEE-key."
The child said, "Ho! Key-key-ma-DEE-key!"
  and she filled her waterpot and set it on her head.
The Crab said, "Don't forget as you are going back!"
  And the child set off along the path.

All the way, she kept saying,
  "Old Woman Key-key-ma-DEE-key, Key-key-ma-DEE-key."
But when she was nearly there, she stumbled,
  and her waterpot fell from her head, broke,
  and all the water ran upon the ground;
  and she went on home.

The old woman said, "Where is the waterpot, Grandchild?"
She said, "As I was coming, I stumbled and it broke."
The old woman said,
  "Take another and go splash water some more."
  The child took another and went back to the river.

When the Crab saw her coming, he said,
  "Why are you back so soon?"
She said,
  "That name you told me, I have gone and forgotten it,
  and I have come back to ask it again."

The Crab said,
  "She is called Old Woman Key-key-ma-DEE-key."
  And the child said, "Ho!"

Then she filled the waterpot, and placing it on her head,
  she hurried back saying the name all the way.
When she reached home, she set down the waterpot,
and the old woman said, as before,
  "Go and dig yams and bring them."

And the child did everything as before:
  prepared food, set it before the old woman, who said,
  as before, "Mention my name and take and eat."

The child said, "You are called Old Woman Grandmother."
The old woman said, "I mean, my real name!"
The child said, "Your real name?"
The old woman said, "Yes."
She said, "You are called Old Woman Key-key-ma-DEE-key!"

At this, the old woman became very angry,
but she said, "Well, take and eat, then!"
    And the child took and ate.

The old woman picked up her calabash,
    "I am going in search of the very one who told you my
                            name," she said.
    And she set off along the path to the river.

First, she met Obonto the Minnow, and she spoke thus:
    "You, 'Bonto, your mother! You, 'Bonto, your father!
    Did you tell my grandchild I am called
                        Key-key-ma-DEE-key?"
The Minnow said, "It was not I."

Next, she saw Adwen the Fish nearby, and she spoke thus:
    "You, Adwen, your mother! You, Adwen, your father!
    Did you tell my grandchild I am called
                        Key-key-ma-DEE-key?"
    The Fish said, "It was not I."

Then she saw the Crab standing nearby, and she cursed him,
    in like manner, saying, "You Crab, your mother!
    mother! mother! You Crab, your father! father! father!
    Did you tell my grandchild I am called
                        Key-key-ma-DEE-key?"

The Crab said, "Yes, it was I. As for you,
 why did you let somebody's child grow so thin?"
This made the old woman very angry,
 and she lifted up her calabash and threw it hard
     at the back of the Crab.

There it stayed on the Crab's back,
 and that is how the Crab got a shell on his back.
Long ago, there was not a shell on the back of a crab.

For his part, the Crab picked up white clay from the
 riverbed and threw it at the old woman's head,
 and there it stayed on the top of her head.

That is why, to this day, on the top of an old woman's
    head there is white hair.

These my stories, which I have told you,
    if they be sweet or if they be not sweet,
    take some with you and let some come back to me.

about the words
Rute Larungu

about the pictures
Lou Turechek

c/o TELCRAFT Books
3800 Mogadore Industrial Parkway
Mogadore, OH 44260

*"He who befriends the leopard need not fear
the deepest forest."*